DATE DUE

DEMCO 38-296

CHEMICAL AND BIOLOGICAL WEAPONS:
Anthrax and Sarin

Gregory Payan

HIGH
interest
books

Children's Press
A Division of Grolier Publishing
New York / London / Hong Kong / Sydney
Danbury, Connecticut

To Casey, my muse

Book Design: MaryJane Wojciechowski
Contributing Editor: Mark Beyer

Photo Credits: Cover © Index Stock; p. 5 © Agence France Presse/Corbis Bettmann; p. 6 © Reuters/HO/Archive Photos; p. 9 © Reuters/Kimimasa Mayama/Archive Photos; p. 10 © Reuters/Steve Marcus/Archive Photos; p. 14 by Angela Booth; p 16 © Telegraph Colour Library/FPG; p. 18 © Corbis; pp. 20, 29, 30, 41 © Corbis/ Bettmann; p. 23 © Reuters/Yun Suk Bong/Archive Photos; p. 24 © Peter Russell/The Military Picture Library/ Corbis; p. 26 © SPL/Custom Medical; p. 33 © Photri; p. 36 © Reuters/Mike Larson/Archive Photos; p. 38 © Reuters/Dept. of Defense/Archive Photos.

Visit Children's Press on the Internet at:
http://publishing.grolier.com

Payan, Gregory.
    Chemical and biological weapons: anthrax and sarin / Gregory Payan.
        p. cm. — (High-tech military weapons)
    Summary: Discusses the components, use, and history of chemical and biological weapons, especially anthrax and sarin, and explains the effects on humans after exposure.
        ISBN 0–516–23337–8 (lib. bdg.) — ISBN 0–516–23537–0 (pbk.)
    1. Anthrax–Juvenile literature. 2. Sarin–Juvenile literature.
3. Biological warfare–Juvenile literature. 4. Chemical warfare–Juvenile literature. [1. Anthrax. 2. Sarin. 3. Biological warfare. 4. Chemical warfare.] I. Title. II. Series.

UG447.8 P38 2000.G46L37 2000
358'.34–dc21   99–058095

CONTENTS

INTRODUCTION

Chemical and biological weapons: The names sound fancy, but the weapons are not. Anybody who understands science can make them. In recent years, terrorists have used these weapons to kill dozens of people. Thousands more have been injured.

Only powerful nations used to own chemical weapons, but not anymore. In fact, two of the most deadly chemical and biological weapons can be easily bought or made. They are sarin and anthrax. Sarin is a chemical weapon. Anthrax is a biological weapon. Both can be made by almost any person in your neighborhood. People who make these weapons want to kill a lot of people quickly and easily.

Terrorists attacked these citizens of Tokyo, Japan, with the nerve gas sarin.

CHAPTER 1

DEADLY WEAPONS USED BY KILLERS

The Aum Shinrikyo (Japanese for "Supreme Truth") is a religious cult. They have their headquarters 70 miles (113 km) outside of Tokyo, Japan. In 1995, this group used sarin to kill dozens of people and injure thousands. Before that, the group tried many times to kill innocent Japanese civilians. The Aum Shinrikyo are terrorists. Terrorists are people who fight against their own and other governments with whose beliefs they don't agree. Terrorists are hard for governments to fight. This is because terrorists can be your

Shoko Asahara is the leader of the Aum Shinrikyo. This religious cult has attacked innocent civilians.

neighbors, or even your friends. These people want to change the way governments rule by using deadly force.

People's worst fears about chemical and biological weapons came true when the Aum Shinrikyo began to terrorize Tokyo. From 1992 to 1995, the Aum Shinrikyo made anthrax and sarin. They wanted to kill thousands of innocent people. Nine different times the group attacked Tokyo citizens using anthrax. None of these attempts to kill people worked. This is because the group used a harmless type of anthrax.

However, on March 20, 1995, the Aum Shinrikyo succeeded in an attack. This time the group used sarin. Members of the cult released sarin into a Tokyo subway. This attack killed twelve people and injured 5,500. This attack marked the first time a terrorist group used a chemical weapon in an attack. Their attack on the Tokyo subway could have

A chemical control unit helps during a sarin attack.

caused many more deaths. However, the group once again didn't do a good job in making their sarin. Soon after the attack, police captured members of the terrorist cult. It was then discovered that future attacks had been planned for New York City and Washington, D.C.

Larry Harris was arrested for having biological weapons that he planned to use against civilians.

ANTHRAX AND SARIN: WEAPONS OF CHOICE

Anthrax is a germ that exists in our natural world. It can also be made into a weapon in a laboratory. Sarin is a chemical that needs to be made using other chemicals. Anthrax and sarin are the most popular types of biological and chemical weapons. Bombs that can spread anthrax or sarin are cheap to make. They are much easier to make than atomic bombs. Knowing only a little about science is enough to make anthrax or sarin.

The information needed to make anthrax and sarin can easily be obtained. Anybody can find out how to make both by doing a little research. This means that the same information is available to terrorist organizations.

Anthrax and sarin give terrorist groups a chance to attack quickly and cheaply. Quick attacks kill many people. The Aum Shinrikyo have proved this. The threat of more attacks is very real. However, not only terrorist groups want to kill people.

Ordinary civilians can also have the same anger at governments or people that terrorist groups have. Larry Harris was an Ohio lab technician. Harris was arrested after trying to purchase ingredients to make biological weapons of his own. Harris was found to be a member of a racist organization. Harris spent time in jail for his criminal activity.

Chemical and biological weapons attacks will increase as more information on buying and making them becomes available. Dangerous civilians or terrorist groups are able to get a lot of information from the Internet. Many illegal books and pamphlets also publish deadly information. The U.S. government fears this. It has tried to stop such easy access to dangerous information. In 1997, the United States spent $42.6 million on a Domestic Preparedness Program. The money will be given to cities around the country. The cities will use the money to pre-pare for terrorist attacks. These cities also are learning to fight such attacks. They fight attacks by finding the people who are buying or making these weapons.

WHAT CAN GOVERNMENTS DO?

Terrorist attacks scare governments all over the world. This is because terrorists kill civilians during peacetime. Civilians are targets that cannot fight back. There have not been many biological or chemical weapon attacks on civilians. Most often, terrorists use bombs to kill people and threaten governments. However, terrorists are much more likely to use chemical or biological weapons than are two nations at war with each other.

For more than sixty years, countries have made biological and chemical weapons. These weapons are among the worst known today. They destroy humans slowly and painfully. Yet many nations continue to spend millions of dollars each year making them. Almost twenty countries can now make chemical and biological weapons. The United States, Russia, England, Canada, and China are among them. Fortunately, they have chosen not to use chemical and biological weapons during wartime. Chemical and biological weapons have, however, been used in past wars.

PAIN RELIEVER   NDC280-2000-50

GENUINE
BAYER ®
ASPIRIN

Fast, Safe Pain Relief
TOLERAID® MICRO-COATING
CAFFEINE AND SODIUM FREE

**USE ONLY IF SEAL UNDER CAP WITH WHITE Bayer
Corporation PRINT IS INTACT.**

INDICATIONS: Fast, safe, temporary relief of
headache pain, muscle aches and pains, pain and
fever of colds, and minor aches and pains of arthritis.

DIRECTIONS: Adults and Children 12 years and over:
take 1 or 2 tablets with water every 4 hours, as
needed. Do not exceed 12 tablets in 24 hours.
Questions? Comments? Please call 1-800-331-4536.

Bayer Corporation,
Consumer Care Division
Morristown, NJ 07960 USA

50 TABLETS *325 mg*   11-7030HW

CHAPTER 2

USING CHEMICALS TO KILL

THE HISTORY OF SARIN

The German drug company, Bayer, first made sarin. Bayer is best known for making aspirin. Sarin is a chemical taken from a different chemical. That chemical is called Tabun. Sarin was first made to kill insects. Today it is used to kill only people.

Sarin is a liquid that has no color or smell. Sarin gives off a colorless, odorless gas. When inhaled, it can be deadly. An amount smaller than the period at the end of this sentence could kill a human being. This means that

Some companies, such as Bayer, produce helpful drugs but also have created deadly chemical weapons.

only a tiny amount of sarin is needed to kill thousands of people. What makes sarin so scary is that it is easy to make. The materials needed to make it are cheap and easy to buy.

Once sarin is sprayed into the air, it quickly disappears. It disappears by drying up. People who are attacked with sarin must inhale it quickly. Otherwise the chemical won't harm them. Because it disappears quickly from the air, the attacker is able to enter into the place where it was used. This makes sarin a good weapon for the military.

BRAIN

HEART

SYMPTOMS AND EFFECTS OF SARIN

Sarin's effects on the body happen fastest when it is inhaled. The lungs contain many thousands

LUNGS

of blood vessels. When inhaled, sarin quickly gets into the bloodstream. Once in the bloodstream, the poison moves to important organs such as the lungs, heart, and brain. These are the organs where sarin can do the most harm. Sarin does less harm when it is absorbed through the eyes and skin. Symptoms (signs that you have been infected) appear quickly. A person can die within a couple of minutes to a few hours. The speed that it takes to harm or kill someone depends on the amount of sarin to which a person is exposed. The part of the body that has absorbed the chemical also can make the difference between injury and death.

When exposed to low levels of sarin, the pupils of the eyes become smaller. A headache occurs. The nose begins to run. More saliva is produced in the mouth. At higher levels of exposure, coughing and sweating occur. Breathing becomes difficult. Soon nausea, vomiting, and blurred vision

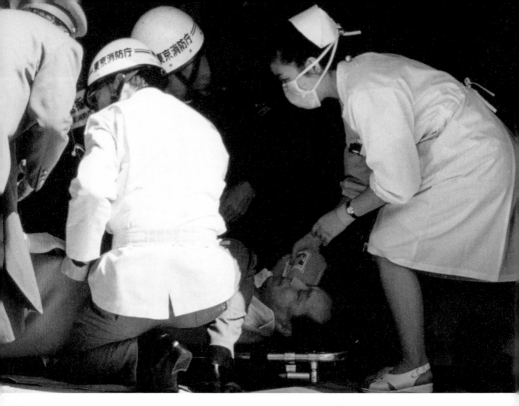

Fast treatment after exposure to sarin can make the difference between life and death.

happen. Blood pressure drops and the victim falls asleep. Sleep happens because sarin harms the brain. The brain is the body's central nervous system. After sleep hits, muscles stop moving. The muscles stop that help the lungs to inhale and exhale. The victim can no longer breathe, and soon death occurs. When huge amounts of sarin are absorbed by the body, death is almost immediate.

CHAPTER 3

SARIN USED IN WAR AND PEACE

Most people believe Iraq used sarin during the Iran-Iraq War (1984–1988). However, the most people killed by a sarin attack happened in the Aum Shinrikyo terrorist attack in Japan. Sarin has been used very little during wartime. However, other chemical weapons have been used during war. Many countries used chemical weapons during World War I (1914–1918). Some types of these weapons include tear gas, mustard gas, and chlorine gas. These weapons killed 91,000 people during the war. They injured another 1.3 million people.

World War I was the only major war in which chemical weapons were used against soldiers.

When sarin was first made in Germany in the late 1930s, the Nazi dictator Adolf Hitler wanted to make a lot of sarin. He wanted to use this chemical against his enemies. He was told by his military experts not to make large amounts of sarin. Until 1945, only a small amount of sarin had been produced. Some people believe that if Hitler had ordered the mass production and use of sarin, Germany could have won World War II (1939–1945). By 1945, German factories started making more sarin. After 1945, the Soviet

Union took control of the German weapons factories and stopped making sarin.

PROTECTION FROM CHEMICAL WEAPONS ATTACKS

Once released, sarin is hard to detect during a battle. This is because today's army troops have special electronic devices that can "breathe" the air. These devices tell the troops whether a chemical weapon has been used.

Cities have no such devices. If used against a city population, the chemical is almost impossible to detect.

Defense is hard against a sarin attack. During an attack, a person must wear a gas mask and protective clothing. If they do not, they will become exposed to the chemical. You've already learned what happens if you are exposed to sarin. It's pretty gruesome.

Military troops carry gas masks and can put on special clothing during chemical weapons attacks. However, almost no civilians own gas masks. Also, it seems unlikely that civilians would want to carry one just in case an attack occurs.

A gas mask fits around the head. It contains a filter with specially treated charcoal to remove vapors. This filter has special paper layers to remove dangerous particles from the air. A suit that covers the body also uses charcoal to protect the skin. The gas mask and suit do a good job of protecting a person. However, masks and suits are hot and uncomfortable. Wearing them makes it hard for soldiers to perform normal duties, such as drive or talk on a radio.

TREATMENT FOR CHEMICAL WEAPONS EXPOSURE

All governments want to protect their citizens. Treating people with drugs before an attack occurs is possible. But the drugs used

Today, soldiers use chemical weapon masks and clothing for protection against such attacks.

today have not been very successful during testing. These drugs are in tablet form. They work best if taken thirty minutes before possible exposure. For a civilian population at risk of an attack, using the pills for protection would fail. It would be nearly impossible to guess when a sarin attack might happen. Also, it would be impossible to get the pills to every person in a city. However, the pills can help military troops.

Taking this pill before a sarin attack gives someone a better chance for survival if exposed. However, it does not prevent harmful symptoms. If the tablets are taken after exposure to sarin, they will make the symptoms of exposure worse. The best protection is to stop the enemy from using chemical weapons at all.

Skin exposed to sarin must be washed. Clothes should be destroyed to prevent others from becoming infected. Immediate medical help is necessary if the person is to have any hope of living. Oxygen must be provided to help the victim breathe.

There is a cure for sarin exposure. This cure (antidote) is to inject the drug atropine. A needle must be stuck into a large muscle, such as the thigh muscle. Soldiers can give themselves a shot if necessary. This antidote helps the body to fight the effects of the sarin. It also helps the nervous system to work until more

The sarin antidote, called atropine, is dispensed with an auto-injection syringe.

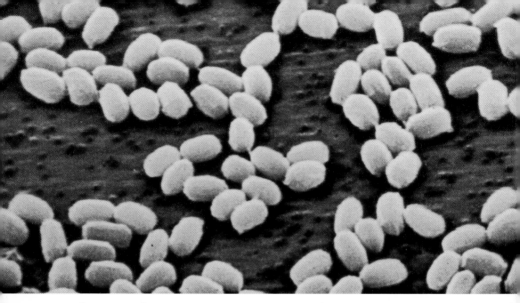

Anthrax bacteria, shown here under a microscope, are found naturally in the environment.

treatment can be given. But if the antidote is given and the person has not been exposed, he or she will become very sick.

Today, a sarin attack during wartime may not work so well for the attacker. Troops wearing gas masks and suits are not at risk. However, the unsuspecting and unprotected civilian population can be harmed. Police organizations such as the Federal Bureau of Investigation (FBI), the Canadian Mounted Police, or Interpol must find terrorist groups before they attack. Only then will innocent citizens be protected from chemical weapons.

CHAPTER 4

ANTHRAX: BACTERIA THAT CAN KILL

Bacteria are living things so small that you must use a microscope to see them. Some bacteria are good and are needed in the environment. Other types of bacteria may cause harmful diseases. Anthrax is a disease caused by the bacterium *anthrax bacillus*. This bacterium is found naturally on Earth. It is also easy to make this bacteria into a weapon. Exposure to some types of anthrax can cause lung damage. Other types of anthrax can be more harmful. If not treated quickly, anthrax can also cause death.

THE HISTORY OF ANTHRAX

People have known about anthrax for more than three thousand years. Anthrax was first written about by the ancient Egyptians. In 1500 B.C., anthrax was responsible for the fifth Egyptian plague. It infected and killed thousands of people. In the Middle Ages (A.D. 500–1500), anthrax nearly destroyed all of the cattle herds of Europe. Animals can become exposed to anthrax from drinking water near soil infected with anthrax. They can also become sick from eating dead animals that are infected.

Anthrax can survive for decades as spores. A spore is a special kind of cell. A spore is not living, but it can grow into a living thing. It is similar to a seed that will become a plant.

In 1871, the German biologist Robert Koch showed that by injecting the spores from anthrax bacteria into a mouse, the mouse would get sick and die. Anthrax was the first

The German biologist Robert Koch was the first scientist to prove that disease came from bacteria.

bacteria found to be a cause of disease. Before that, diseases were mysteries which could not be explained.

In 1881, the French chemist and biologist Louis Pasteur developed a form of the anthrax vaccine. A vaccine is a substance that protects the body against disease. Here's how it works. A tiny bit of the bacteria or virus that causes the disease is injected into a person. The bacteria will purposely infect the person. This infection is so weak that it isn't even harmful. However, by becoming infected with a weak virus, an immunity to the disease is created. Once immune, a person cannot become infected by the disease.

SYMPTOMS AND EFFECTS OF ANTHRAX

Most people will never come into contact with anthrax. People are almost never exposed to anthrax in the United States and Canada. However, when these cases do occur, they can be very harmful. After exposure to anthrax, symptoms appear one to seven days later. These symptoms differ depending on the type of anthrax poisoning. Humans can be exposed to anthrax in three ways: through the skin, by eating meat from an infected animal, or by breathing in spores.

Cutaneous Anthrax

Anthrax exposure through the skin is called cutaneous anthrax. Cutaneous means "of the skin." This kind of anthrax enters the body through a cut or an open sore in the skin. Cutaneous anthrax is the most treatable form of the disease. At first, there is an itchy skin

Louis Pasteur, a French chemist, developed the anthrax vaccine to protect the body from the disease.

infection that looks like an insect bite. Within one or two days, it becomes a painless bump with a black center. This is called an ulcer. The ulcer gets worse until the victim is very sick. Usually large doses of the antibiotic penicillin are given to fight the disease. Only 20 percent of untreated cases of cutaneous anthrax will cause death. Death is very rare in cases in which the victim is treated.

Intestinal Anthrax

Intestinal anthrax occurs when a person eats contaminated meat, or drinks contaminated milk (from an animal that has anthrax.) This type of anthrax is hard to treat. The symptoms include flu-like aches and pains and stomach cramps. Severe skin infections and difficulty breathing also occur. There is swelling of the intestines, followed by nausea, vomiting, and fever. Stomach pain, diarrhea, and vomiting of blood also occur during later stages of the disease. Once discovered, intestinal anthrax must be treated with heavy doses of antibiotics. Death occurs in 25 percent of untreated cases.

Inhalation Anthrax

Breathing anthrax into the lungs causes the most fatal form of the disease. This is called inhalation anthrax. Inhalation anthrax occurs when anthrax spores are breathed directly into the mouth, throat, and lungs. Anthrax spores are colorless and odorless. A person cannot know if he or she has inhaled the spores.

The first symptoms of inhalation anthrax may feel to a

Large doses of penicillin, a natural antibiotic, must be taken to fight some types of anthrax poisoning.

person as if he or she has a cold. After the spores enter the lungs, they change into bacteria and begin to produce poisons. The poisonous bacteria are spread throughout the body by the bloodstream. As the disease spreads, breathing becomes more difficult. The toxins cause bleeding in the lungs first. Then organs, such as the liver, kidneys, and stomach, begin to bleed. Soon after, the infected person dies. Inhalation anthrax is nearly untreatable after symptoms have begun. It is very deadly and is the most likely type of anthrax to be used by terrorists.

Something You Should Know

Scientists have figured out a frightening detail. A small plane carrying only 220 pounds (99 kg) of anthrax spores and flying over Washington, D.C., on a clear, calm night could release those spores and kill between one and three million people.

ANTHRAX VACCINE AND TREATMENT

The vaccine for anthrax is made from a harmless part of the anthrax bacteria. The human body is able to tell that the bacteria are anthrax. Therefore, the body fights the bacteria with cells that attack the dangerous bacteria. These cells are called antibodies. After fighting off this harmless type of anthrax, the antibodies are able to fight off the deadly types of anthrax. The antibodies help the body's immune system by stopping the bacteria from making deadly poisons. The vaccine for humans was developed in the 1960s. It was approved for use by the Food and Drug Administration (FDA) soon after. Since 1970, people whose jobs bring them into contact with anthrax have been vaccinated. These are people such as lab workers, veterinarians and livestock handlers. For thirty years, the anthrax vaccine has been safely used to protect people at risk.

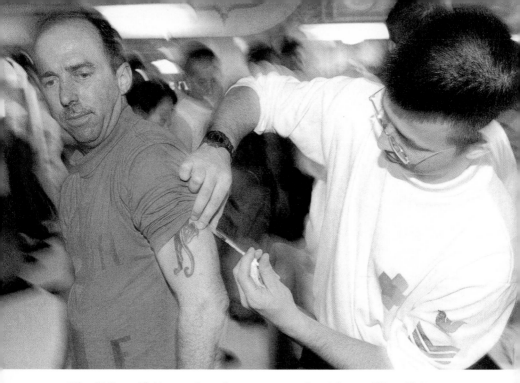
The U.S. military has begun vaccinating all military personnel for anthrax.

In 1998, U.S. Secretary of Defense William Cohen approved the plan to vaccinate all military personnel for anthrax. The entire U.S. armed forces will be vaccinated by 2003. For 99 percent of unprotected people, exposure to anthrax spores would kill them. Yet the disease is almost harmless to those vaccinated. Both the United Kingdom and Canada also plan to vaccinate their armed forces in the near future.

CHAPTER 5

ANTHRAX USED IN WAR AND PEACE

During World War II, the Allies (the United States, Britain, France, and Russia) thought about using anthrax against German troops. However, they decided not to use biological weapons against their enemies. Luckily for all humanity, anthrax has never been used during a war.

During the 1980s, inspection teams discovered that Iraq had produced 2,000 gallons (about 8,000 liters) of anthrax spores. This is enough anthrax to kill every man, woman, and child on Earth.

This aerial photograph shows a chemical weapons storage facility in Iraq.

In April 1979, the largest number of deaths caused by anthrax occurred in Sverdlovsk, Russia. Anthrax was released, and sixty-six people died. For years, the former Soviet Union said contaminated meat caused the deaths. In fact, it happened as a result of biological weapons research. It wasn't until 1994 that the newly formed government of Russia admitted their crime. They admitted to the people that government testing was responsible for the deaths of their citizens.

DIFFICULT TO USE

Anthrax and other biological weapons are very difficult to use during combat. Because of wind direction and the terrain (shape of the land), it is hard to keep biological weapons from infecting just one area. These weapons can affect such large areas that civilians are as likely to become infected as are enemy military troops.

Powerful nations such as the United States and Russia have trained armies to use anthrax and other biological weapons. These armies have also been trained to survive a biological attack by another nation. Many nations spend millions of dollars each year to continue their research and development of anthrax. The United States, Britain, Russia, Japan, and others all have experimented with anthrax in recent years.

MUST CHEMICAL WEAPONS EXIST?

All nations that attended the Biological Weapons Convention of 1972 signed an agreement. That agreement was supposed to stop production of all chemical and biological weapons. The United States helped to create this international treaty. The United States, the Soviet Union, and more than one hundred other nations signed that treaty. However, nearly thirty years later, nobody believes that any nation is keeping its promise to stop making these weapons.

What would happen if the United States put aside the money spent each year on weapons development? Well, it could help the homeless problem. That money could

The Biological Weapons Convention of 1972

also be used for some other need, such as improving our education system. However such money could be used, it is now wasted on making newer and more deadly chemical weapons. There is a possibility the information needed to make these weapons and to buy their ingredients will fall into the hands of dangerous individuals, groups, or terrorists. Then the whole world is put at risk.

absorb to take in or hold

antibiotic a substance used to fight infection or disease

antidote a medicine that acts against the harmful effects of a poison

biological weapon a weapon using bacteria or viruses as its method of killing

chemical weapon a weapon using a chemical compound as its method of killing

civilian a person who is not a member of any armed force

cult a group of followers devoted to a person or belief

cutaneous of the skin

immunity resistance to disease or poison

Interpol an international police organization which works with many nations to stop crime

livestock farm animals

respiration the act of breathing

syringe a device or tube, usually with a needle on one end, used to inject fluids into, or to draw fluids out of, the body

terrain the natural features of an area of land

terrorists people who use terror or violence to intimidate

vapor a gas formed by a substance that is usually a liquid or a solid

FOR FURTHER READING

Corvisier, Andre. *A Dictionary of Military History*. Malden, MA: Blackwell, 1994.

Dunnigan, James. *How to Make War: A Comprehensive Guide to Modern Warfare for the Post-Cold War Era*. New York: William Morrow, 1993.

Levine, Herbert M. *Chemical and Biological Weapons in Our Time*. Danbury, CT: Franklin Watts, 2000.

Meltzer, Milton, and Sergio Martinez. *Weapons & Warfare: From the Stone Age to the Space Age*. New York: Harper Collins, 1996.

RESOURCES

Centers for Disease Control and Prevention
Department of Health and Human Services
1600 Clifton Road, NE Mailstop D14
Atlanta, GA 30333
Web site: *www.os.dhhs.gov*

United States Department of Defense
Assistant Secretary for Public Affairs
The Pentagon
Washington, D.C. 20301
Web site: *www.defenselink.mil*

Web Sites
The Organization for the Prohibition of Chemical Weapons
www.opcw.nl
This is the official Chemical Weapons Convention Web site. It includes information about their goals and the worldwide chemical weapons problem. You can also find educational information about the dangers of various chemical and biological weapons.

RESOURCES

Anthrax Vaccine Immunization Program
www.anthrax.osd.mil
On the Defense Department's official anthrax Web site, you'll find information on anthrax and its harmful capabilities. There are links to other sites that offer information about anthrax, its use, and controlling terrorist organizations that may use the agent against the public.

INDEX

INDEX

About the Author

Gregory Payan is a freelance writer living in Queens,
New York.